BLUE ANGELS

The Blue Angels are one of just three official U.S. military display teams. The others are the Army Golden Knights and Air Force Thunderbirds.

BLUE ANGELS

HIGH FLYERS

CAROLINE "BLAZE" JENSEN

CREATIVE EDUCATION · CREATIVE PAPERBACKS

Published by Creative Education and Creative Paperbacks
P.O. Box 227, Mankato, Minnesota 56002
Creative Education and Creative Paperbacks are imprints of The Creative Company
www.thecreativecompany.us

Book Design by Tom Morgan
Art direction by Blue Design (www.bluedes.com)

Images by Unsplash/Peter Pryharski, 4–5, 32; Wikimedia Commons/Balon Greyjoy, 25, Mass Communication Specialist 2nd Class Cody Hendrix/U.S. Navy, 26, MC1 Rachel McMarr/U.S. Navy, 21, MC2 Andrew Johnson/U.S. Navy, 12–13, MC3(SW) Travis K. Mendoza/U.S. Navy, 30, National Museum of the U.S. Navy, 11, Petty Officer 1st Class Jessica Pielop/U.S. Navy, 20, Petty Officer 2nd Class Kathryn Macdonald/U.S. Navy, 18, PH1 CHUCK MUSSI, 6, PH2 Paul O'Mara, USN, 2, public domain, cover, 1, 8, public domain, 7, ScottMLiebenson, 22, U.S. Navy, 14, 15, 16, U.S. Navy Petty Officer 2nd Class Michael Hight, and a privatemuse, 29

Library of Congress Cataloging-in-Publication Data
Names: Jensen, Caroline, author.
Title: Blue Angels / by Caroline "Blaze" Jensen.
Description: Mankato, Minnesota : Creative Education and Creative Paperbacks, [2026] | Series: High flyers | Includes bibliographical references and index. | Audience: Ages 10-13 | Audience: Grades 4-6 | Summary: "The U.S. Navy's Blue Angels showcase the precision and power of naval aviation. Soar high with the air display team, in this visually stunning introduction to their history, present, and future, geared toward upper-elementary readers" — Provided by publisher.
Identifiers: LCCN 2025015272 (print) | LCCN 2025015273 (ebook) | ISBN 9798895810620 (library binding) | ISBN 9798896800156 (paperback) | ISBN 9798895811887 (ebook)
Subjects: LCSH: United States. Naval Flight Demonstration Squadron—Juvenile literature. | Stunt flying--Juvenile literature. | Aeronautics, Military—Juvenile literature.
Classification: LCC VG94.6.N38 J46 2026 (print) | LCC VG94.6.N38 (ebook) | DDC 797.5/40973—dc23/eng/20250512
LC record available at https://lccn.loc.gov/2025015272
LC ebook record available at https://lccn.loc.gov/2025015273

Printed in the United States

ABOUT THE AUTHOR — Caroline "Blaze" Jensen flew 3,600 hours in the Air Force as a fighter pilot, including F-16 combat missions and Thunderbirds demonstrations. She lives in Wisconsin with her son, Finn, and dog, Gunner. She loves sharing her passion for flying with kids of all ages.

Blue Angels pilots endure up to 7.5G's.

CONTENTS

WING TIPS

Formed in 1946, the the Blue Angels are the second oldest official aerobatic team in the world. ↗

HIGH FLYERS

Flying with the Angels

Have you ever seen jets zooming overhead, so close they could almost touch? If they were painted navy blue with yellow letters, you saw the amazing Blue Angels! The Blue Angels are a highly trained team of pilots who perform tricks and stunts at airshows all summer. They fly at lightning-fast speeds, make tight turns, and fly within inches of each other. Sometimes, they even fly upside down! Their perfect formations wow crowds and make people wonder, "How do they do that?"

The Blue Angels return home to Naval Air Station Jacksonville in Florida after a show in 1947.

The U.S. Navy started the Blue Angels just after World War II to show off the skill of its pilots and the abilities of its planes. Since 1946, the Blue Angels have become one of the most famous flying teams in the world. They share the skies with the U.S. Air Force Thunderbirds, the Canadian Snowbirds, the United Kingdom's Red Arrows, and others.

The Blue Angels are more than jets flying amazing tricks. Nearly 300 demonstration pilots and thousands of support crew are part of their legacy. Team members are carefully selected. They train for hours to ensure all the tricks—called maneuvers—are done safely. Blue Angels serve a two- to four-year tour depending on their position. The pilots are very experienced when they are selected for the team. They fly at high speeds, do sharp turns, and handle high G-forces—which make them feel up to seven times heavier than they are!

The team works hard because it represents all members of the Navy. It helps the Navy sign up recruits and shows off the professionalism and pride of being part of the Navy to an estimated 11 million people at more than 30 shows each year.

If you are excited to learn more, you are in luck! Put on your golden helmet and strap in! You are cleared for takeoff!

THE U.S. NAVY

The U.S. Navy has a long and proud history. It started in 1775 during the American Revolution to protect the shores and help with trading. Over the years, the Navy has been involved in many wars: World Wars I and II, Korea, Vietnam, Iraq, and Afghanistan. The Navy is also important in peacetime, helping with aid after natural disasters. Sailors serve on ships and submarines and work on aircraft to help keep peace worldwide. The Navy values honor, courage, and commitment.

3
163765
U.S

Blue Angels aircraft can return to combat duty aboard aircraft carriers within 72 hours.

An F8 Bearcat aircraft of the Blue Angels in 1946

Blue Angels' Beginnings

Admiral Chester Nimitz

Admiral Chester Nimitz was an important Navy leader. He was in charge of the U.S. Pacific Fleet in Pearl Harbor, Hawaii, during World War II. He stayed calm and made good decisions to help the Navy fight back against the attacking Japanese fighters. He helped the United States win the War in the Pacific after many fierce battles with Japanese forces.

Admiral Nimitz approved the creation of the Blue Angels in 1946. He wanted to show off the skill and power of Navy aircraft. He believed it was a great way to show them to Americans who lived in the middle of the United States and couldn't

The Blue Angels have flown 10 different aircraft models since 1946. ↓

see the Navy bases on the coasts. The Blue Angels quickly became popular for their exciting airshows.

One of the most famous Blue Angels was Captain Roy "Butch" Voris, the first flight lead and officer in charge of the Blue Angels. He became a fighter ace in World War II after shooting down eight enemy aircraft. Captain Voris selected the aircraft that the Blue Angels would fly and the pilots and maintenance crew from the best officers and sailors in the Navy. He also chose the blue and gold paint that people still see today. The team picked the name "Blue Angels" because it was the name of a famous New York nightclub.

The Blue Angels have flown several aircraft over time, including the F6 Hellcat, F8 Bearcat, F9 Panther (below), and F9 Cougar. The F-11 Tiger was the aircraft in

WAR ANGELS

When wartime called, the Blue Angels answered. During the Korean War, their aircraft, pilots, and some crew members joined a fighter squadron nicknamed "Satan's Kittens." Sadly, their leader was shot down and killed during combat. Today, the Blue Angels do not fly in combat as part of their tour, but most pilots have flown combat missions before joining the team.

the first six-plane demonstration. At the end of the 1960s, the Blue Angels flew the F-4 Phantom. The F-4 Phantom was flown by both the Blue Angels and Air Force Thunderbirds in their demonstrations. The F-4 was also one of the main aircraft flown during the Vietnam War. The Blue Angels often had to send parts to Vietnam to ensure that the Navy fighter jets had the parts needed to fly missions. They then turned to the Eglin Air Force Base in Florida to get other parts to continue flying their airshows. They switched to the A-4 Skyhawk in 1974.

By 1986, the team started flying the Navy's F/A-18 Hornet. In 2021, they transitioned to the F/A-18 Super Hornet, which is bigger than the previous version of the Hornet. The Super Hornet is 25 percent larger and can fly 40 percent farther than the Hornet.

Lieutenant Commander Amanda Lee made history as the first woman pilot in the Blue Angels' F/A-18 demonstration. She flew in the 2023 and 2024 airshow seasons. Her first season was also the 50th anniversary of women flying in the Navy. Lieutenant Commander Lee worked as a crew chief on the F/A-18 Hornet earlier in her career.

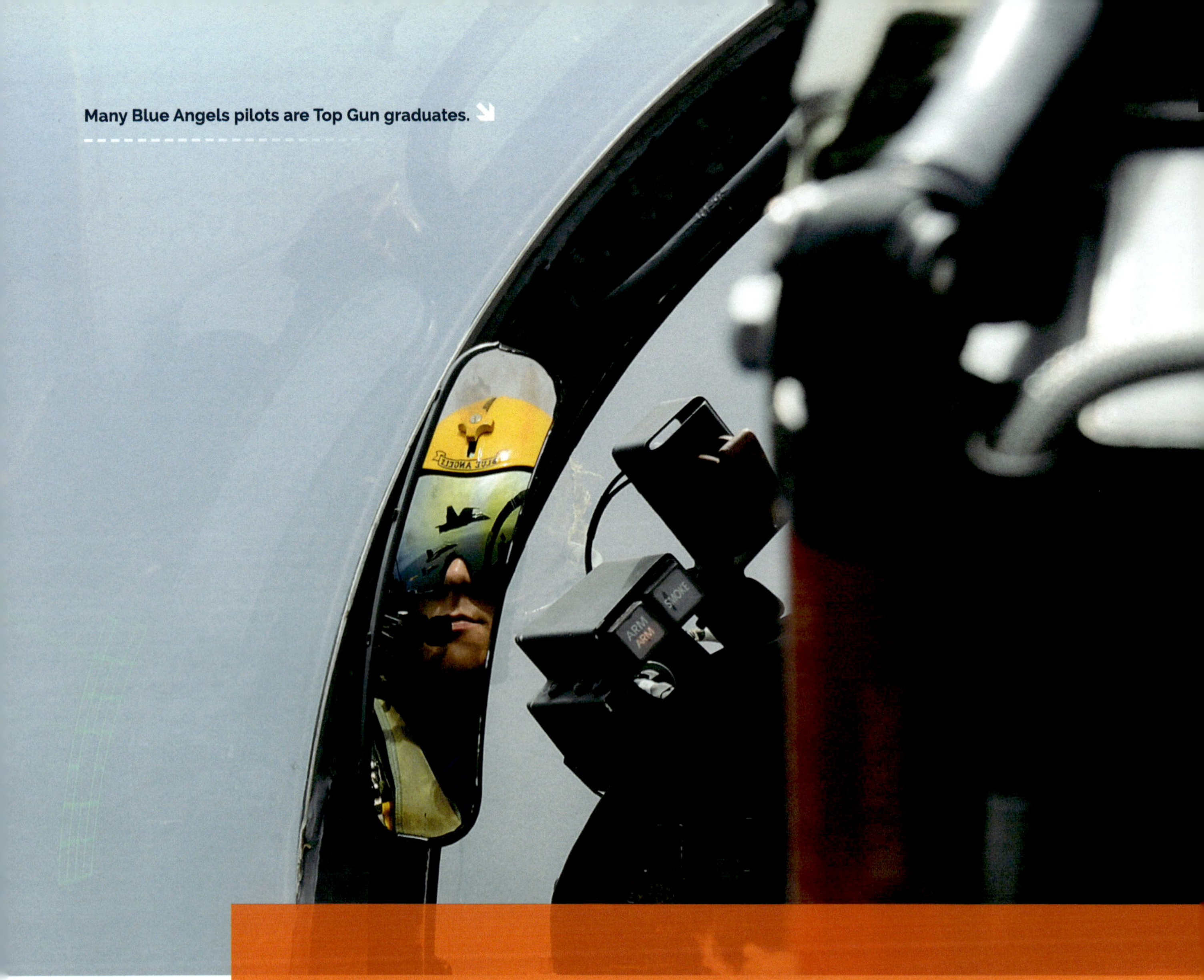

Many Blue Angels pilots are Top Gun graduates.

HIGH FLYERS

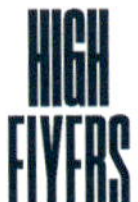

TOP GUN

Top Gun is a special training program for top Navy pilots. Pilots learn how to use their jets against enemy jets. They fly simulated fights to test their teamwork and decision-making skills. Top Gun is famous for training the best pilots. Many Blue Angels pilots are Top Gun graduates.

HIGH FLYERS

Becoming a Blue Angel

Becoming a Blue Angel is a dream for many who love jets and serving their country. To join the team, people need to be dedicated, hard workers, and very good at their jobs. Kids who want to become Blue Angels should work hard in school, avoid drugs and illegal activities, and stay active in sports or physical fitness. They should also focus on activities where they can be leaders and learn new skills.

There are more than 150 active-duty sailors and Marines on the team, including 16 officers. Each year, the team selects three fighter pilots, two support officers, and one Marine Corps

The C-130J, also called "Fat Albert"

C-130J Super Hercules pilot to replace those who leave at the end of their tour. The selection process is very tough. Once selected, pilots go through special training to learn the famous Blue Angels stunts.

The officers include six demonstration pilots and a pilot narrator who tells the crowd what the team is doing during the show. There are also an event coordinator, an executive officer, and three pilots who fly the C-130J, called "Fat Albert." The C-130J transports the team and equipment to airshow locations. Other officers include the maintenance officer, flight surgeon (team doctor), supply officer, and public affairs officer. Each year, only one Marine officer flies in the F/A-18 airshow. All three pilots flying the C-130J are Marine Corps pilots.

The number 7 jet is special. The team selects people from the community they visit to fly in the back seat of a Super Hornet! These lucky civilians are public figures, leaders of youth organizations, teachers, guidance counselors, or school employees. They share the experience with others.

The support team sends about 45 members to each show site. The commanding officer recommends these team members for the special assignment. They are on the team for three years. The Blue Angels could not fly airshows without the non-flying team members who do dozens of other jobs to make the team successful.

Becoming a Blue Angel takes a lot of time, effort, and dedication. But it is a very rewarding job. If you love flying and want to be part of a team that excites millions of people, this could be the job for you!

GUEST OF THE ANGELS

Lucky guests who get to fly with the Blue Angels do not fly in formation with all six jets. They do many of the stunts, but as just one jet. With good weather and permission from air traffic control, the guest gets a "max climb takeoff." The pilot lights the afterburner and zooms to 10,000 feet (3,048 meters) within seconds. Guests fly before the airshow so they can share the story on social media or the news. Flying different people at each airshow location helps attract the public to the airshow.

The Blue Angels help the public learn about the Navy.

The Blue Angels fly in precise formations.

HIGH FLYERS

Training for a Safe Show

Once selected, pilots go into intense practice. They start flying in El Centro, California, in November for two months. Then they fly from Pensacola, Florida, for two more months. Pilots need to fly 120 training flights to perform the stunts safely. They start with easier tricks, flying higher above the ground. As they improve, they add more jets to the formation and fly lower when it is safe.

Flying a safe show is very important. Pilots must protect the people watching them. It is also important that the pilots stay safe, and the aircraft, which cost about $67 million each, are kept safe. A Blue Angels pilot must be brave. It is a very dangerous job. Twenty-eight Blue Angels have lost their lives in flying accidents during practices and airshows. The Blue Angels practice to look good but mostly to ensure safety for pilots and spectators.

Even though the Super Hornet can pull 7.5G's, the pilots do not wear a G-suit. When the pilot pulls G's, blood rushes to the lower part of the body. This is bad because humans need blood flow to their head for their brain to work. A G-suit helps keep the blood in the brain. But when pilots fly, they rest their arm on their leg. If a G-suit were there, it would inflate and deflate, moving their arm around. Pilots want to stay steady when flying as close as 18 inches (45.7 centimeters)

'PULLING G'S'

G stands for "gravity." It is the force that pulls things down toward Earth's surface. When a pilot "pulls G's," the jet changes direction rapidly. G's measure the force on the pilot's body and the jet's ability to maneuver. We feel 1G on Earth, but if the jet pulls 2G's, it feels like twice the normal gravity. Heavy arms on a rollercoaster during loops and spins are an example of G-forces.

The Blue Angels can fly very close together.

from another airplane. To keep the blood flow to the brain, they flex their leg and stomach muscles.

Team members spend a lot of time away from their homes and families while with the Blue Angels. They have a busy practice schedule. Team members support one another while away. People in their communities help support the families back home.

The Blue Angels perform around 70 shows at 34 locations across the United States each year.

HIGH FLYERS

The Show

The airshow season starts in March and goes through November each year. The Department of Defense gets requests for the Blue Angels and makes sure the team has everything it needs for the airshow. Then, the squadron looks at the requests and decides which shows to attend. The Blue Angels fly most of their shows in the United States, but they have also performed in Canada, Europe, and Asia.

The Blue Angel Super Hornets have some special features not found on combat Super Hornets. There is no gun on the Blue Angel. Instead, the planes have smoke oil tanks that allow them to trail beautiful white smoke while flying. The smoke helps the pilots see each other during the show and helps the crowd see the jets and tricks. The oil is natural and turns into smoke when it hits the heat of the exhaust. No oil floats down to the crowd. These special jets are also updated to fly upside down longer than a normal Super Hornet. Even though the jets are different, they can be ready for combat on an aircraft carrier within three days.

The Blue Angels need at least 3 miles (4.8 kilometers) of visibility and clouds higher than 8,000 feet (2,438 meters) to do the most popular version of their show. They have three different versions of the show to fly if there are clouds. If the clouds are really low, about 2,000 feet (609.6 m) above the ground, the planes can safely perform only level maneuvers in front of the audience. If the clouds are a little higher, they can do rolls and upside-down maneuvers. If the weather is really good and the skies are clear, they can do all the tricks, including loops and high-up maneuvers. The highest maneuver in an airshow is a Vertical Roll that can go up to 15,000 feet (4,572 m). The lowest maneuver is a Sneak Pass that can be as low as 50 feet (15 m) above the ground.

The Blue Angels fly slower than the speed of sound to avoid a sonic boom, which can shatter glass and windows! The slowest speed flown is 120 miles (193 km) per hour in a maneuver called the "high alpha." The jet flies past the crowd with the tail down and nose up.

The Blue Angels use oil to create smoke trails for visibility and safety.

The fastest the Blue Angels fly during an airshow is 700 miles (1,126.5 km) per hour.

FASTER THAN SOUND

A sonic boom is the loud sound a plane makes when it flies faster than the speed of sound. It makes a big boom, like a clap of thunder. The speed of sound is how fast sound travels through the air. The speed of sound is 767 miles (1,234.4 km) per hour. When airplanes break the sound barrier low to the ground, the sonic boom can break windows. The pilots must be careful not to fly faster than the speed of sound.

When we see the Blue Angels fly, their skill and bravery remind us that we can do great things when we have great teammates.

When the six jets fly together in a formation, it's called the "delta." When you see four aircraft flying in a close formation, it's called the "diamond." The diamond is made up of the leader, the left wingman, the right wingman, and the slot pilot who flies directly behind and underneath the leader. The diamond pilots are numbers 1 through 4. Numbers 5 and 6 are the solo pilots. They fly passes between formation maneuvers from the diamond pilots.

The Sneak Pass is one of the crowd's favorite maneuvers. It surprises everyone when an F/A-18 flies by very fast from behind, without the audience knowing it's coming! The fastest speed is about 700 miles (1,126.5 km) per hour. Another favorite maneuver is the Double Farvel. In it, the tight diamond flies with two jets upside down. The flight leader and the slot pilot fly inverted as they pass the crowd. The Dirty Loop is a loop flown with the gear and flaps down. Many people also enjoy the opposing solo passes, when two jets come from opposite sides and look like they may hit each other because they appear to pass so close.

Whether the Blue Angels are flying in tight formations or performing near-miss maneuvers, they always show teamwork. They inspire many people to set big goals and work hard to reach them. When we see the Blue Angels fly, their skill and bravery remind us that we can do great things when we have great teammates.

INDEX